The Adventures Of Bob The Bat

The Adventures Of Bob The Bat

D. Scott Davis

The Adventures Of Bob The Bat

A children's book

By D. Scott Davis

Copyright pending 2021

Woodsong Publishing
5989 Spring Meadow Lane
Seymour, IN 47274

Woodsong books may be ordered at:
www.woodsongpublishing.com

Woodsong books may also be ordered through various online retailers.

Illustrations by Eliza Wilson

Cover design by Vision Graphics

Printed in the United States of America

ISBN: 978-1-7349323-9-3

Thank you
to my wonderful wife,
amazing daughter,
son-in-law,
and granddaughter.

Thank you for all the bat
experiences that made this possible.

The Adventures Of Bob The Bat
By D. Scott Davis

Bob was a little Brown bat that lived in a little red barn on a small farm. The little red barn sat on top of the hill that looked down on Big Town.

Since bats only come out at nighttime, Bob would spend his days inside the barn, hanging upside down from a nail that stuck out from the ceiling.

But when the sun would start to slide down behind the silhouette of Big Town, and evening time would arrive, Bob would jump down from his perch and fly out of the barn. He would swoop and dive around the light that hung outside the barn where he lived.

Bob would chase the mosquitoes and other flying bugs, which Bob found to be very tasty meals, since bats eat insects. Bob knew that the barn-light attracted lots of bugs, so he knew it was the place to be when his stomach started to growl and rumble from hunger. Bob was happy and free. His life seemed complete, and to the other animals that Bob shared the little red barn with, they would all agree that Bob was the happiest bat on the farm.

But when darkness was complete and quiet fell across the farm, Bob would land to rest on the rusty weathervane that teetered atop the little red barn. As Bob reclined against the metal rooster that decorated the top of the weathervane, he would look out at the lights of Big Town.

The streetlights and neon signs from Big Town gave up a glow that put Bob in some sort of strange trance.

Bob thought if one simple light hanging from the front of his barn attracted a bunch of bugs, just think about all the bugs that must be flying around the flow of the light from Big Town. Bob was sure that if the little light on his barn would attract the big, tasty bugs Bob liked to eat, he was sure that the great big lights of Big Town would mean the biggest and plumpest insects that he could only dream about it.

So, the next evening, Bob woke up at sunset and started flying towards Big Town. As the night got darker, the lights of the town flowed even stronger and seemed to pull Bob right to the middle of Big Town. Bob did not realize how far away Big Town was from his little farm on the hill. But Bob was determined and kept flying towards Big Town without evening stopping to catch his breath or to find a beetle to snack on along the way.

Finally, Bob arrived at the edge of Big Town. Bob was so surprised by what he saw. The lights were even brighter than what he had seen from the weathervane on top of his little red barn back on the farm. The colors seemed to flow from the lighted signs and beaming fixtures in an endless light show. The buildings were so big that Bob could hardly believe his eyes when he compared them to the little red barn back home on the farm on the hill.

By now, Bob was getting hungry since he did not stop to even eat a mosquito on his flight to Big Town. So off he flew around the bright lights of Big Town looking for the big juicy bugs that he had dreamed about while peering down on Big Town from the little red barn back on the farm.

But Bob did not find the bugs he was hoping for to fill his tummy. Streets and sidewalks surrounded the big buildings and shiny lights of Big Town. Where was the grass? Where were the weeds and wildflowers? How was any bug able to live under these conditions? How was a bug able to live in Big Town at all, Bob thought to himself? So, Bob decided that if he could just find a nice meadow, like the one next to his barn back home, that he would surely find something to eat.

Off Bob flew above Big Town, looking for the perfect spot to find that perfect bug for his first perfect meal in Big Town. Bob swooped and swayed through the buildings until he came across some houses.

The lights were not as bright as what he first found when he came to Big Town, but they still burned brighter than the one little light that hung from his barn back home. The houses had carpets of fresh cut grass and carefully groomed flowerbeds. Some even had little gardens that gave off the sweet scent of turned soil just like back home on the farm. Bob climbed high in the sky and made a big sweeping turn towards a street light next to one of the houses. Bob could see the shimmer of bug wings fluttering under the light as he zipped down out of the darkness.

Bob tried to open his mouth as big as the barn door back on the farm so he could get as many bugs as possible in at one time because he was so hungry. As Bob dashed through the glow of the streetlight, the bugs and insects filled his mouth to overflowing. Bug legs and insect wings stuck out of the corners of Bob's mouth as he flew away from light. Bob swallowed up his mouthful of bugs without even taking the time to chew up his dinner.

Wow, Bob thought to himself! The bugs were even tastier than he had imagined back on the farm. Bob continued to fly and eat and eat and fly, as the night grew older and older. Bob was so thrilled with the bright lights and tasty bugs that he had found in Big Town.

By now, Bob was getting tired. His trip to Big Town had taken longer than what he planned and all those insects he ate, without chewing them up properly, made Bob's stomach twist and ache. Sunrise was on its way and Bob knew he had to find a nice dark barn soon.

But Bob did not find any barns in Big Town. He searched the neighborhoods where he had flown about during the night, looking for just the right place to stop for the day and rest until nighttime came back again. The sky was getting lighter and brighter, and Bob knew he was running out of time.

Just when Bob was about to give up hope, he saw a big old house that seemed to be empty. The lawn looked like it had not been cut recently, and there were lots of old bushes growing around the front porch. Line and lines of ivy were twisting around themselves up one side of the house.

As time quickly started running out for him, Bob decided that he could not be too picky about where he slept. So, he flew around the big old house until he found a loose board that opened to a big dark attic.

Well, it is not like the little red barn back home on the farm, Bob said to himself, but he was tired, and he knew he could not stay out during the daytime. Bob found a dusty brick on the chimney there in the attic and decided that was just the right spot to end his adventure for the night.

So there Bob stayed, hanging from the brick. Bob hardly moved a wing all day. He was so tired. He dreamed of the bright lights and the big, sweet bugs that he found around the houses in Big Town.

As he slept, a smile crept across Bob's little, bat face. Bob seemed happy and content. He might just like it here in Big Town.

CPSIA information can be obtained
at www.ICGtesting.com
Printed in the USA
BVHW020945030122
625356BV00005B/597